The Rainforest Ecosystem

Kids' Earth Science Book Grade 4 |
Children's Environment Books

BABY PROFESSOR
EDUCATION KIDS

First Edition, 2020

Published in the United States by Speedy Publishing LLC, 40 E Main Street, Newark, Delaware 19711 USA.

© 2020 Baby Professor Books, an imprint of Speedy Publishing LLC

Baby Professor Books are available at special discounts when purchased in bulk for industrial and sales-promotional use. For details contact our Special Sales Team at Speedy Publishing LLC, 40 E Main Street, Newark, Delaware 19711 USA. Telephone (888) 248-4521 Fax: (210) 519-4043.

10 9 8 7 6 * 5 4 3 2 1

Print Edition: 9781541959576
Digital Edition: 9781541962576
Hardcover Edition: 9781541979963

See the world in pictures. Build your knowledge in style.
www.speedypublishing.com

TABLE OF CONTENTS

Humans and animals need water to survive.

Have you ever walked into a grocery store and marvelled at the array of food available? Have you ever thought about the fact that you can drink water straight from a faucet? All animals need certain things to survive, such as food, water, warmth and shelter. In society, we have worked together to get access to resources we need.

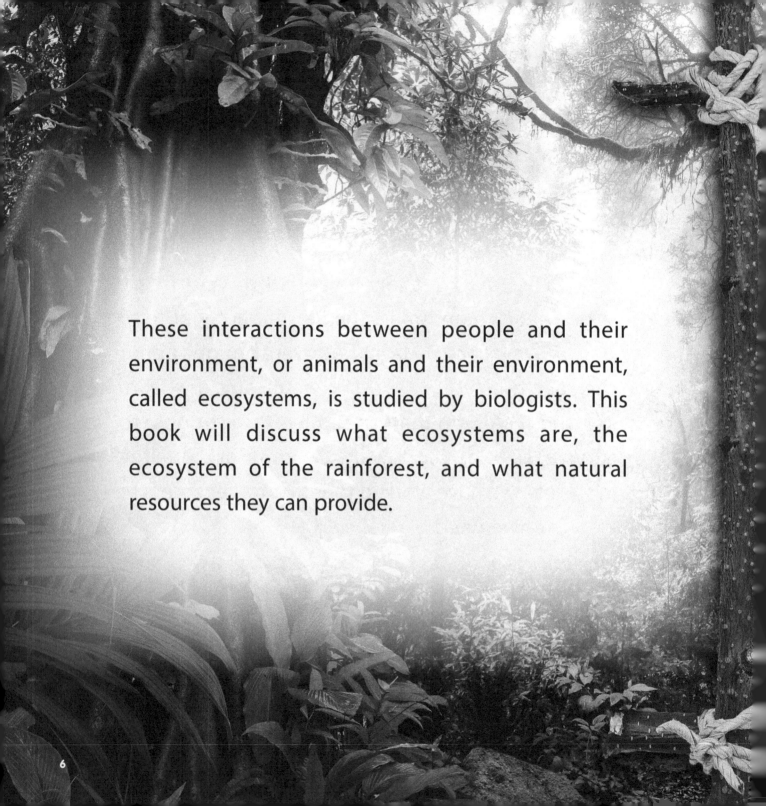

These interactions between people and their environment, or animals and their environment, called ecosystems, is studied by biologists. This book will discuss what ecosystems are, the ecosystem of the rainforest, and what natural resources they can provide.

A biologist studies ecosystems.

CHAPTER ONE:
An Ecosystem

Gazelles eat grass. Lions eat gazelles. This is a basic food chain. However, in order to stay alive, animals must have more than simply food. They need a water supply. They need shelter and the right temperature. Biologists study how these needs are supplied. A disruption that prevents animals from getting what they need for survival not only affects animal and plant life, but also the entire planet. We are only one part of a delicate system.

A lion eating a gazelle is one part of a food chain.

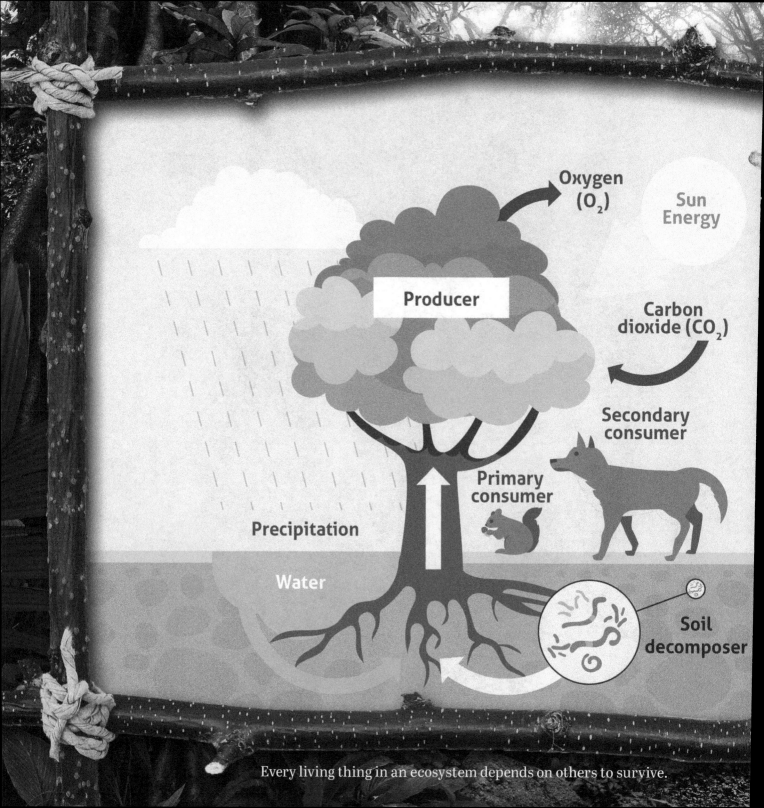

Oxygen (O$_2$)

Sun Energy

Producer

Carbon dioxide (CO$_2$)

Secondary consumer

Primary consumer

Precipitation

Water

Soil decomposer

Every living thing in an ecosystem depends on others to survive.

What is an Ecosystem?

An ecosystem is defined as the interactions of organisms with each other and their environment. Every living thing in an ecosystem depends on others to survive. Living things interact with non-living things in an ecosystem in order to get shelter, food and warmth.

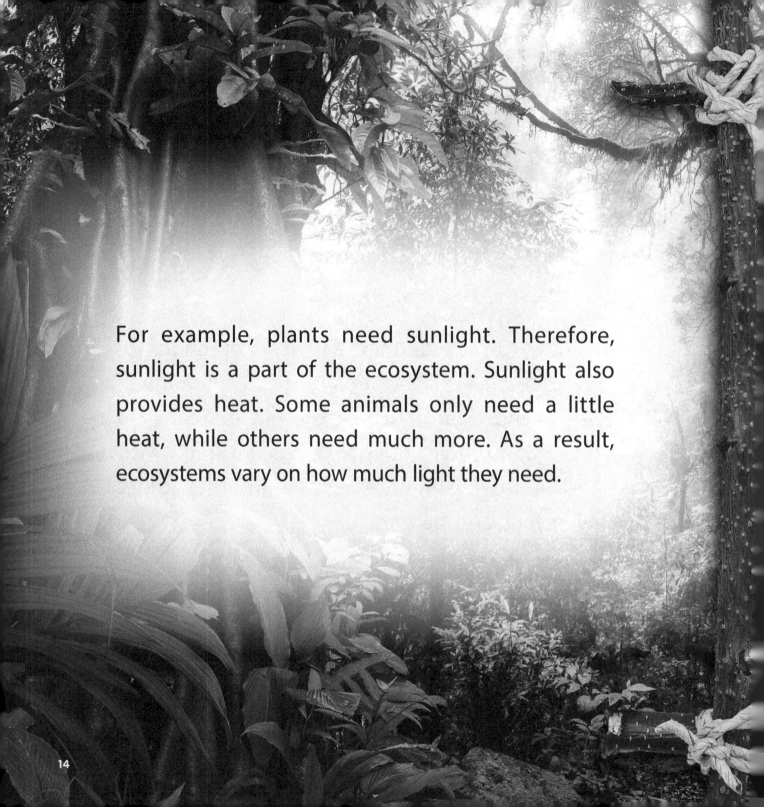

For example, plants need sunlight. Therefore, sunlight is a part of the ecosystem. Sunlight also provides heat. Some animals only need a little heat, while others need much more. As a result, ecosystems vary on how much light they need.

Sunlight is a part of the ecosystem.

The amount of sunlight can also affect the kind of shelter available. Is it a desert? Perhaps the animals burrow underground.

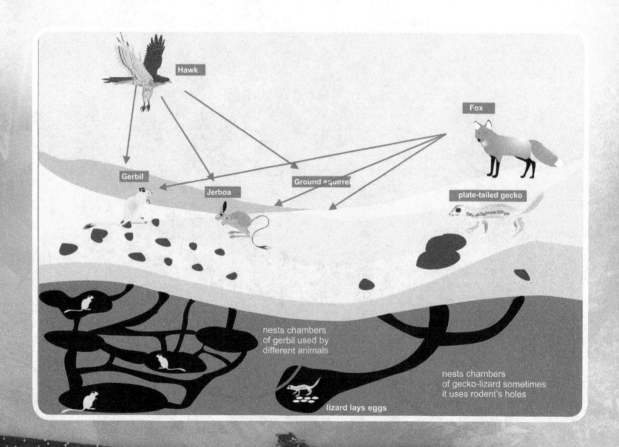

Hawk

Fox

Gerbil

Jerboa

Ground squirrel

plate-tailed gecko

nests chambers of gerbil used by different animals

nests chambers of gecko-lizard sometimes it uses rodent's holes

lizard lays eggs

Desert ecosystem

Is it a forest? Perhaps the animals live in the trees. Perhaps they eat leaves or use the wood to build homes. Both living and non-living things affect each other in each unique ecosystem. The result is a community of healthy organisms.

Forest habitat of animals

Ecosystems come in all different shapes and sizes. They can be so small that they may fit under a rock, or they can be an entire pond.

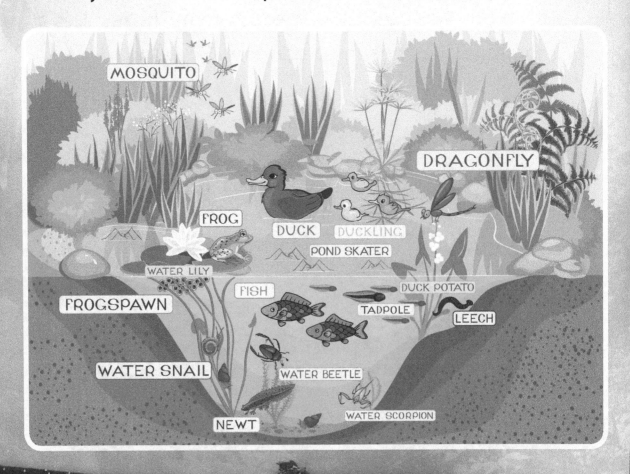

Ecosystem of a pond

At its largest, an ecosystem can be the entire Ocean, or even the entire planet! Ecosystems on land are called terrestrial, while ecosystems in the water are called aquatic.

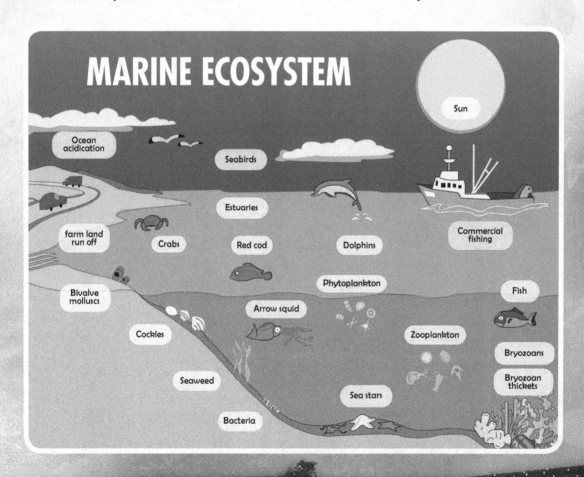

Marine Ecosystem

2 POPULATION

3 BIOCENOSIS

6 BIOSPHERE

4 ECOSYSTEM

1 ORGANISM

5 BIOMA

Illustration of the hierarchy of biological organization

How is an Ecosystem Organized?

To make it easier to study and understand, biologists have organized different levels of an ecosystem. The smallest part that makes up an ecosystem is an individual, which is simply one plant, animal, insect or another organism. A population is made up of individuals who live in the same area, are from the same species, and interact with each other. Next is the community where populations interact within the same area. Finally, all together, they make up an ecosystem where they interact with each other and their environment.

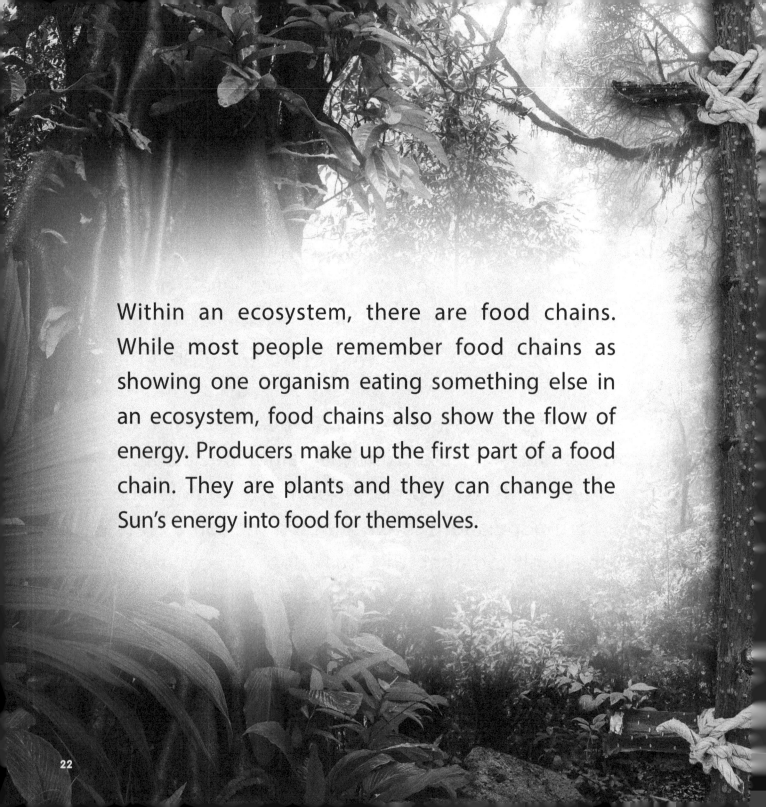

Within an ecosystem, there are food chains. While most people remember food chains as showing one organism eating something else in an ecosystem, food chains also show the flow of energy. Producers make up the first part of a food chain. They are plants and they can change the Sun's energy into food for themselves.

Food web, trophic levels and energy flow

Energy

Food chains also show the flow of energy.

FOOD CHAIN

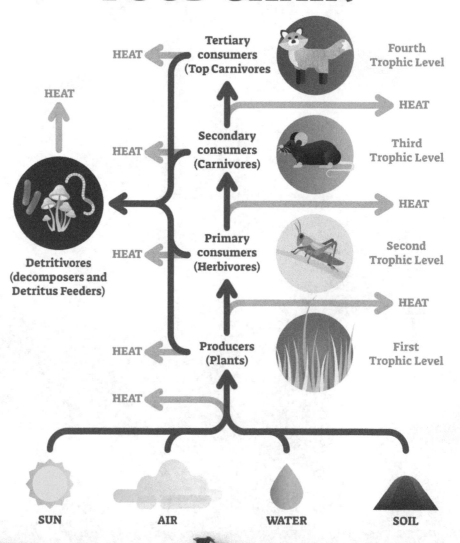

There are different types of consumers based upon how far up the food chain they are.

Anything that eats the producer is a consumer. A consumer can also eat other consumers. There are different types of consumers based upon how far up the food chain they are. A primary consumer eats the producers. The secondary consumers will eat the primary consumers. The different levels of consumers are called trophic levels. By eating plants or other animals, the consumer gets energy to survive. Hence, a food chain shows where the energy goes. Finally, when plants and animals die, they are eaten by decomposers who break down the dead organic material into nutrients for the soil. These nutrients in the soil help plants grow and keep the cycle going.

CHAPTER TWO:
A Rainforest Ecosystem

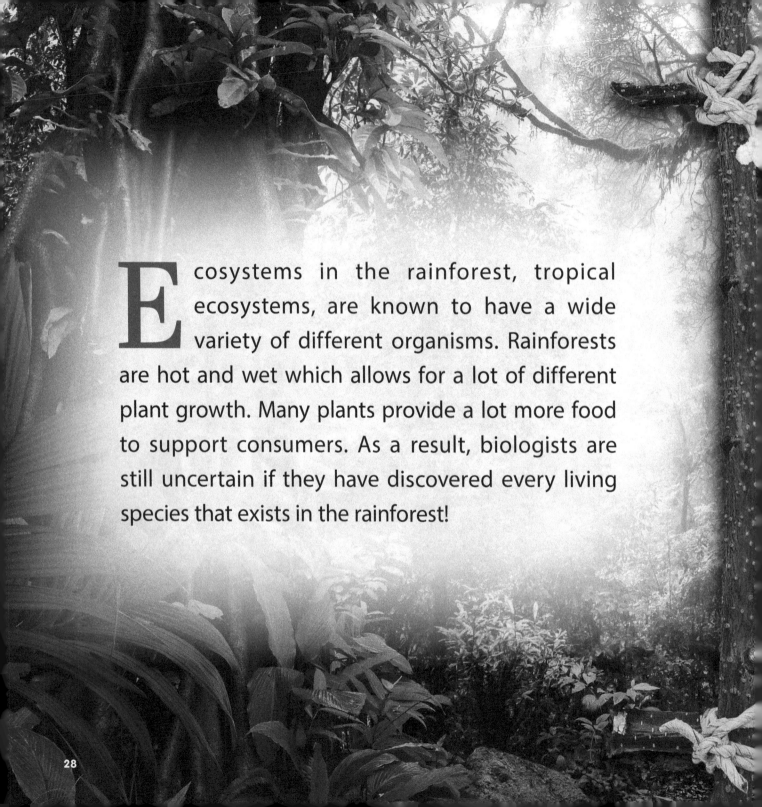

E cosystems in the rainforest, tropical ecosystems, are known to have a wide variety of different organisms. Rainforests are hot and wet which allows for a lot of different plant growth. Many plants provide a lot more food to support consumers. As a result, biologists are still uncertain if they have discovered every living species that exists in the rainforest!

Rainforest in Queensland, Australia

Rain storm over rainforest, Essequibo River Region 9,
Iwokrama, Rupununi, Guyana, South America

Features of the Rainforest:

For a forest to qualify as a rainforest, seventy-five inches of rain is needed in a year. That is over six feet! What is even more incredible is that most rainforests will get a lot more rain than that, about one-hundred inches per year. At their wettest, rainforests will receive over two-hundred and fifty inches! In addition to a lot of rain, rainforests are always hot, typically between seventy, and ninety degrees Fahrenheit. This makes for a very humid environment.

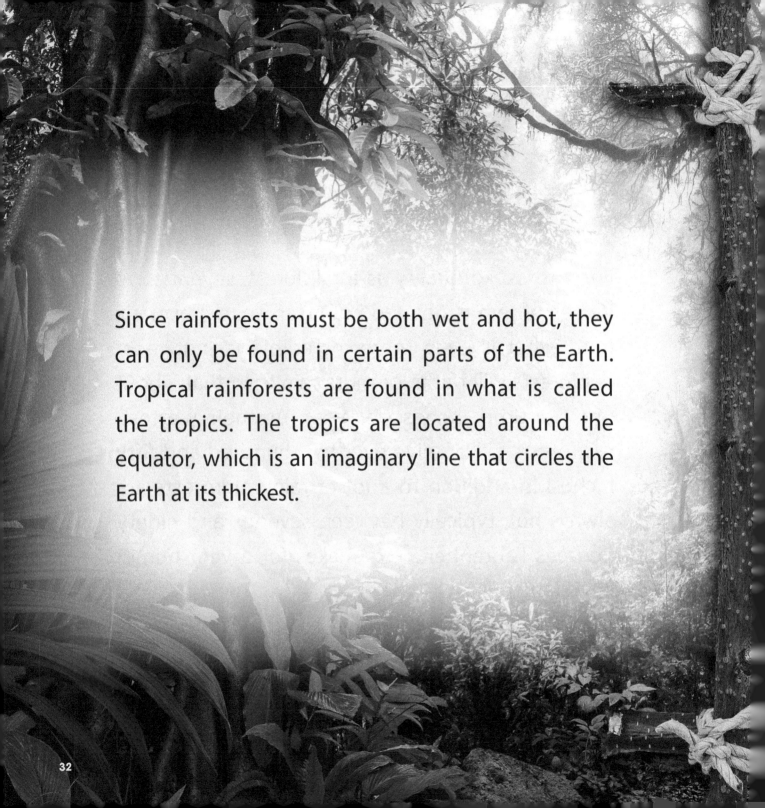

Since rainforests must be both wet and hot, they can only be found in certain parts of the Earth. Tropical rainforests are found in what is called the tropics. The tropics are located around the equator, which is an imaginary line that circles the Earth at its thickest.

Tropical Rainforest in Malaysia

Aerial view of the Amazon Rainforest in Brazil

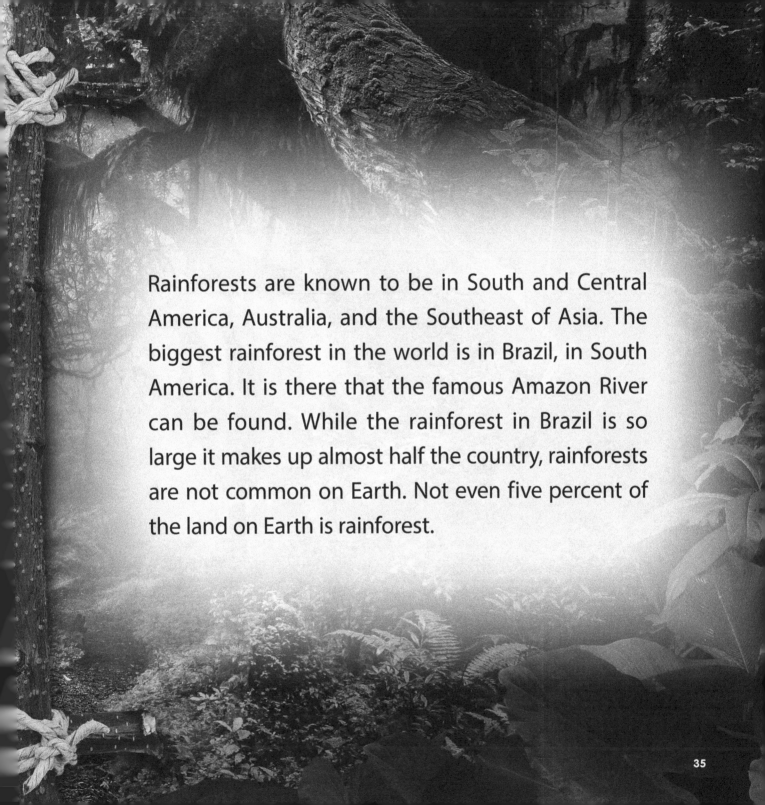

Rainforests are known to be in South and Central America, Australia, and the Southeast of Asia. The biggest rainforest in the world is in Brazil, in South America. It is there that the famous Amazon River can be found. While the rainforest in Brazil is so large it makes up almost half the country, rainforests are not common on Earth. Not even five percent of the land on Earth is rainforest.

Emergent layer ☼ -100% 50-80m

Canopy layer ☼ -95% 30-50m

Understory layer ☼ -5% 1-30m

Forest floor ☼ -2%

Illustration of the layers of a rainforest

Within a rainforest, there are several layers. At the very top, between 100 and 170 feet, there is a layer called the canopy. It is made up of the branches and leaves of tall trees. These branches interlock so thickly that little sunlight will ever reach the forest floor.

Looking up at a rainforest canopy in Osa Peninsula, Costa Rica

Some exceedingly tall trees may grow up over the canopy. These trees are called emergent trees since they "emerge" over the top.

rainforest with emergent Trees visible in Danum Valley, Sabah, Borneo

Underneath the canopy is the understory which is just smaller trees, some shrubs and other plants. The smaller trees rarely get enough sunlight thanks to the canopy and, as a result, never reach their full size.

Palm tree growing in the rainforest understory, Ecuador

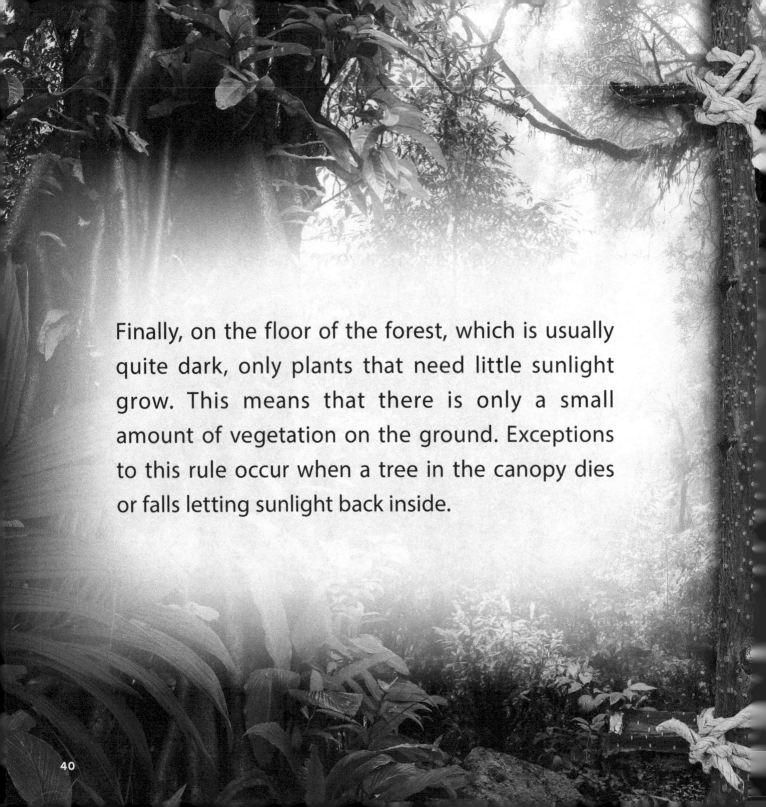

Finally, on the floor of the forest, which is usually quite dark, only plants that need little sunlight grow. This means that there is only a small amount of vegetation on the ground. Exceptions to this rule occur when a tree in the canopy dies or falls letting sunlight back inside.

Rainforest floor in Serrania de San Blas, near
Burbayar Nature Reserve in Panama

Vines thriving on the trunks of tall trees.

Who are the Producers of a Tropical Rainforest?

The producers in the rainforests are known to be incredible. Many of the trees are massive in girth and height. Some plants can attack and eat creatures. There are climbing vines that cling to trees, and flowers the size of large bicycle tires! While trees may shed their leaves at times, they stay green all year around.

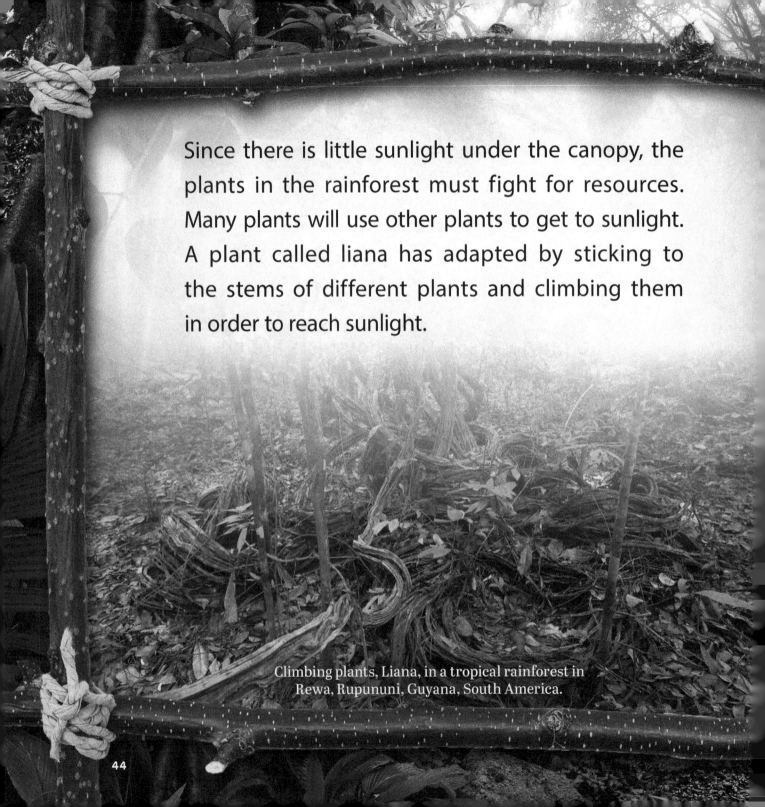

Since there is little sunlight under the canopy, the plants in the rainforest must fight for resources. Many plants will use other plants to get to sunlight. A plant called liana has adapted by sticking to the stems of different plants and climbing them in order to reach sunlight.

Climbing plants, Liana, in a tropical rainforest in Rewa, Rupununi, Guyana, South America.

Epiphytes are a kind of plant that do not get nutrition from the ground. Instead, they live off other plants by getting food and water from them. They also collect rain, and things that are found in the surrounding area.

Epiphytes growing on trees for support, Minnamurra Rainforest Centre, New South Wales, Australia

A lot of plants in the rainforests provide us with medicines.

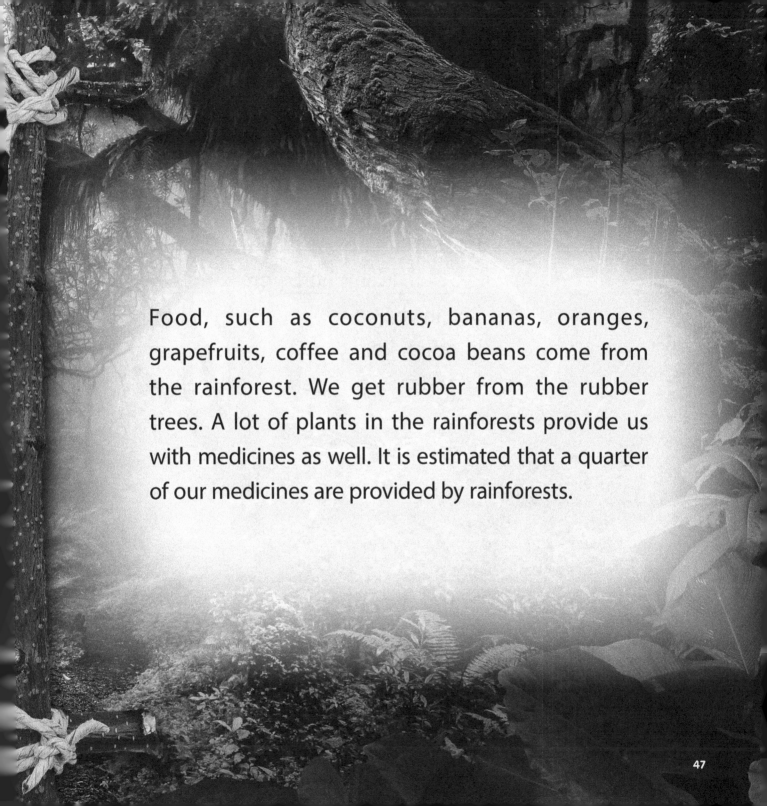

Food, such as coconuts, bananas, oranges, grapefruits, coffee and cocoa beans come from the rainforest. We get rubber from the rubber trees. A lot of plants in the rainforests provide us with medicines as well. It is estimated that a quarter of our medicines are provided by rainforests.

Who are the Consumers of a Tropical Rainforest?

The rainforest has an abundant number of consumers as well. Many herbivores, animals who eat plants, live in the canopy. These include flying squirrels, woodpeckers, and monkeys. Some of the birds, like toucans and parrots, are colorful and well-known.

A monkey sits on a bough of a tree in the forest canopy, Son Tra Nature Reserve, Vietnam.

Red-and-Green Macaws in flight over forest canopy in Buraco das Araras, Jardim, Mato Grosso do Sul, Brazil.

A Yellow-throated Toucan in the Tropical Forest Canopy of Central America.

In the understory and on the forest floor, there are many kinds of animals too. Some examples are gorillas, elephants, pigs, and leopards. A lot of animal species in the rainforests are unique. There are poisonous frogs, sloths, ants that could eat you alive, and many more!

leopard hunting in tropical rainforest in Java, Indonesia

Blue Jeans Dart Frog in Costa Rica's rainforest.

A sloth bear climbing a tree in the Amazon rainforest, near Iquitos, Loreto, Peru.

CHAPTER THREE:
Natural Resources

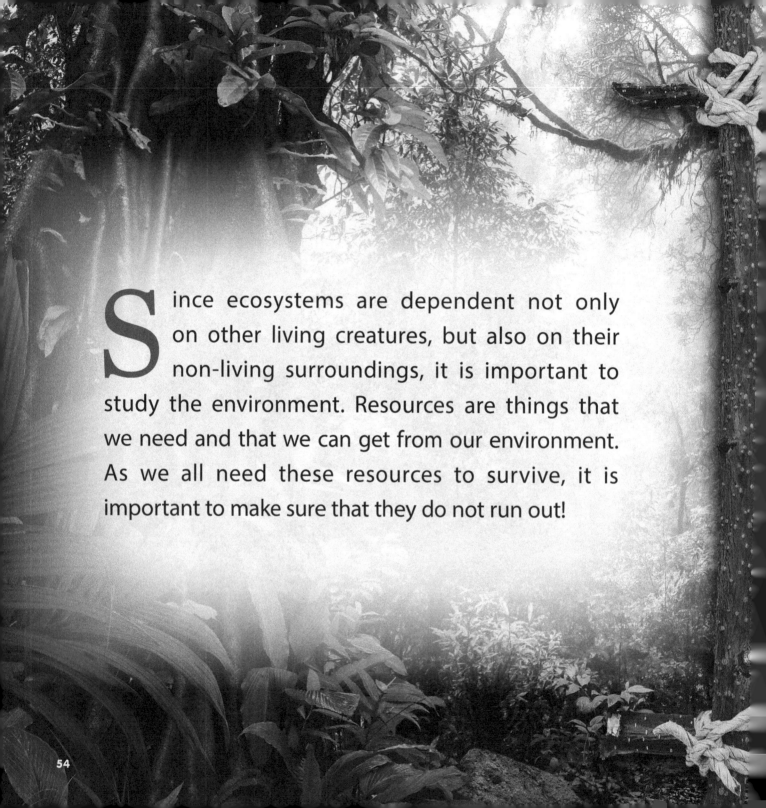

Since ecosystems are dependent not only on other living creatures, but also on their non-living surroundings, it is important to study the environment. Resources are things that we need and that we can get from our environment. As we all need these resources to survive, it is important to make sure that they do not run out!

Natural resources are things that we need and that we can get from our environment.

Coal is a non-renewable resource from fossilized plant matter that is used extensively in homes and industries.

What are Natural Resources?

Natural resources are any resources found on the Earth that are not made by people. They can be either renewable or non-renewable. Non-renewable resources mean that there is a limit on how many or how much are available. Air, water, and minerals, like some that are found in the soil, are all non-renewable because we cannot make more of them.

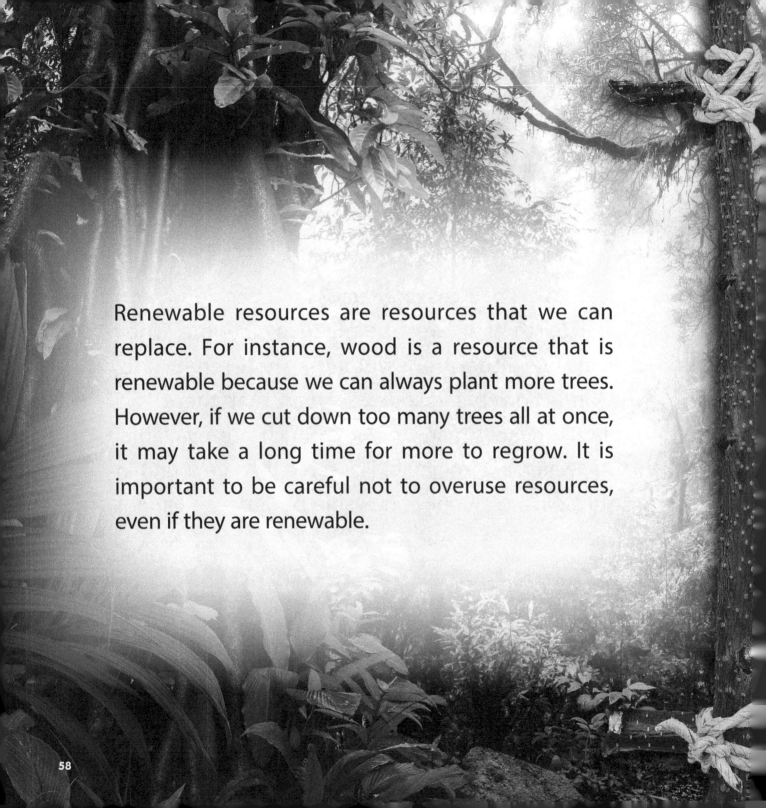

Renewable resources are resources that we can replace. For instance, wood is a resource that is renewable because we can always plant more trees. However, if we cut down too many trees all at once, it may take a long time for more to regrow. It is important to be careful not to overuse resources, even if they are renewable.

Wood is a resource that is renewable because we can always plant more trees.

Why are Tropical Rainforests Important?

Tropical rainforests are important because they provide lots of our food, wood, medicine and other resources. Medicine from the rainforests can help treat simple things like a fever or even more deadly diseases like cancer. Scientists believe that there are still many more medicines to be discovered.

Aboriginal rainforest food found in the Daintree Rainforest in Queensland, Australia

Bellyache bush growing in the Amazon Rainforest of Peru has many medicinal uses.

The berries of the Devil's Club plant, growing in the Great Bear Rainforest of British Columbia, Canada are a native remedy.

Tropical rainforests are also useful in that they help maintain control of our non-renewable resources. Since rainforests have so much plant life, they do a lot of work converting carbon dioxide in the air into oxygen that we can breathe. Without the rainforests, the air quality would not be as good.

Conversion of Carbon Dioxide by trees to Oxygen.

Also, rainforests help maintain the water supply. They take in a lot of water from rain and then release it back into the air. Excess water is also placed into rivers and streams which help provide water to drink and grow crops on farms. Interfering in the rainforest would interfere in the water cycle.

Rainforest river in the Garden of Eden, Gunung Mulu National Park, Sarawak, Malaysia.

If people strip away natural resources greedily, they can cause a great deal of harm.

How are Tropical Rainforests Affected Negatively?

Unfortunately, not everyone has respected the rainforests. Humans, as a part of the ecosystem, affect what happens to the world around them. If people strip away natural resources greedily, they can cause a great deal of harm. Some animals and plants in the rainforest are believed to have gone extinct as a result.

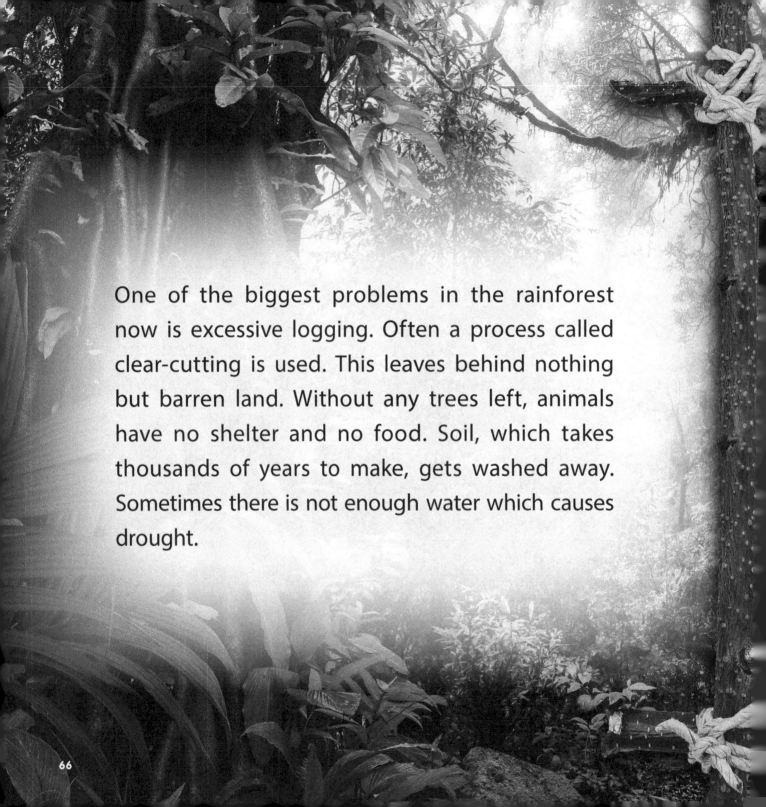

One of the biggest problems in the rainforest now is excessive logging. Often a process called clear-cutting is used. This leaves behind nothing but barren land. Without any trees left, animals have no shelter and no food. Soil, which takes thousands of years to make, gets washed away. Sometimes there is not enough water which causes drought.

Deforestation of tropical rainforests causes harmful long-term effects.

People are encouraged to remember to plant more trees if they have cut some down.

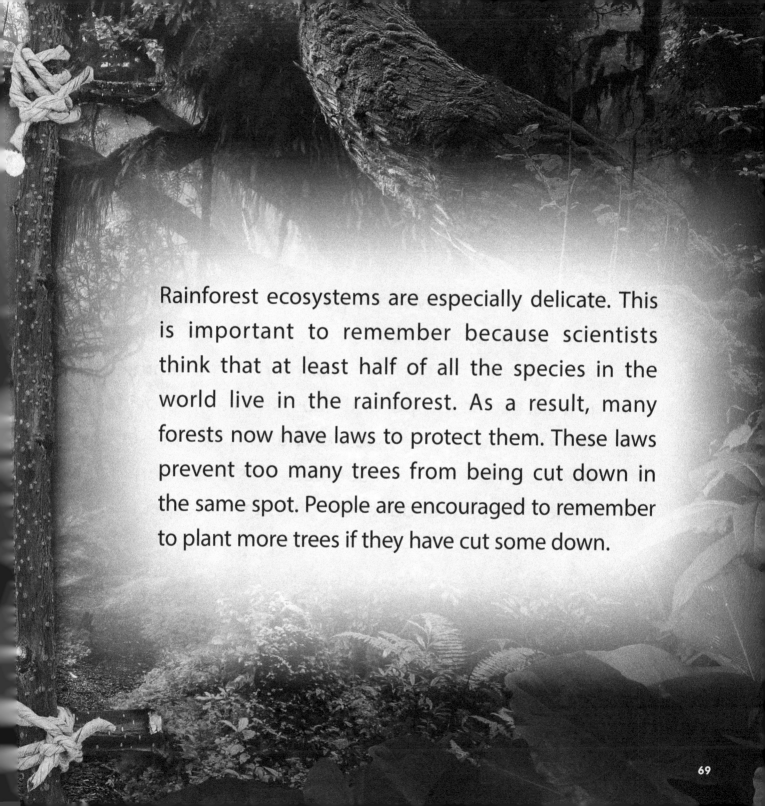

Rainforest ecosystems are especially delicate. This is important to remember because scientists think that at least half of all the species in the world live in the rainforest. As a result, many forests now have laws to protect them. These laws prevent too many trees from being cut down in the same spot. People are encouraged to remember to plant more trees if they have cut some down.

Everyone in the world is part of an ecosystem. An ecosystem is when different species interact with each other and their environment. The rainforest is a particularly important ecosystem as it provides us with many things we need and helps preserve our non-renewable resources. It is important to remember to treat our environment with respect.

Visit

www.speedypublishing.com

To view and download free content on your
favorite subject and browse our catalog of new
and exciting books for readers of all ages.

Printed in the USA
CPSIA information can be obtained
at www.ICGtesting.com
LVHW081949120923
757796LV00021B/2